YOU'RE IN TROUBLE

FIB OR TRUTH?

You Choose the Ending

by Connie Colwell Miller • illustrated by Victoria Assanelli

Do you ever wish you could change a story or choose a different ending?

IN THESE BOOKS, YOU CAN!

Read along and when you see this:

WHAT HAPPENS NEXT?

Skip to the page for that choice, and see what happens.

In this story, George breaks his mother's lamp. Will he tell her the truth? Or will he lie? YOU make the choices.

George wants play ball with his friends, but it's raining.
He tosses a ball in the house. The rule at George's house
is that balls belong outside. George forgets.

George throws the ball as high as he can.
The ball bounces and knocks over his mother's
lamp. SMASH! CRASH! Oh, no!

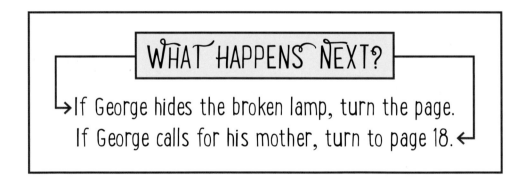

WHAT HAPPENS NEXT?

→If George hides the broken lamp, turn the page.
If George calls for his mother, turn to page 18.←

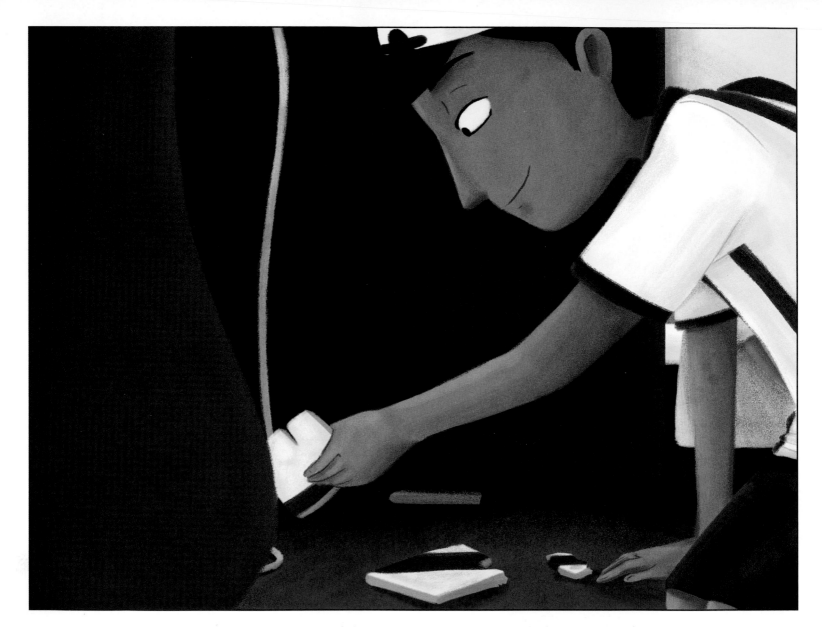

George is scared he will get in trouble. He hides
the broken lamp pieces. Soon, Mom rushes into the
living room. "What was that crash?" Mom yells.

WHAT HAPPENS NEXT?

→ If George tells a fib, turn the page.

If George tells his mother the truth, turn to page 14. ←

"I don't know," George lies. "I didn't hear anything." Mom looks around. "Where is my lamp?" she asks.

WHAT HAPPENS NEXT?

→ If George fibs again, turn the page.
If George tells the truth, turn to page 16. ←

George thinks fast. He doesn't want to get in trouble. "Thomas knocked it over! He broke it!" Mom knows Thomas is too small to reach the lamp. "George, are you telling the truth?"

TURN THE PAGE →

11

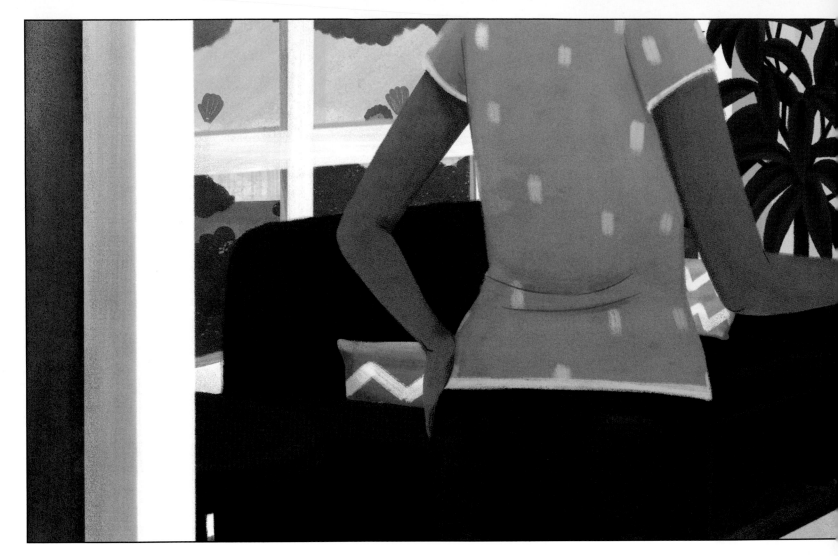

"Yes, Mom," George lies. But Mom finds the pieces. She says, "George, first, you threw a ball in the house and broke the lamp. Then, you hid the pieces. Worst of all, you lied to me. Three bad choices—you are grounded for three days."

Now the sun is out. But George can't go outside to play
with his friends. He should have told his mom the truth.

THE END

→ Go to page 23. ←

"I'm sorry, Mom. I was playing ball and broke your lamp."
George shows her the broken pieces.

"Why did you hide your mistake?" Mom asks.

"I was afraid you would be angry with me," George says.

"Maybe so, but the truth is always better," Mom says.

TURN TO PAGE 20 →

14

"I'm sorry, Mom," George says. "I don't know why I lied. I broke the lamp." "Please go to your room and think about telling the truth," she says.

Now the sun is out, and George can't go outside and play.
He wishes he had told his mom the truth from the start.

THE END

→ Go to page 23. ←

"Mom!" George calls. She was already on her way.

"What happened?" she asks.

George has tears in his eyes. "Mom, I'm sorry. I was playing ball in the house, and I broke your lamp."

TURN THE PAGE →

"You know that you're not supposed to play ball in the house, George. I'm disappointed that you broke a rule," Mom says, "but thank you for telling me the truth. Will you help me clean it up?"

"Mom, I'm sorry. I'll use some of my allowance money to help buy a new lamp," George says.

TURN THE PAGE →

George is sorry he broke the lamp, but he's glad he told his mom the truth. And since the rain has stopped, George finally gets to play ball with his friends—outside.

THINK AGAIN

- What choices did you make for George? How did that story end?
- Go back to page 3. Read the story again and pick different choices. How did the story change?
- Have you ever lied? What happened?

We are all free to make choices, but choices have consequences. Would YOU tell the truth if you did something you weren't supposed to do?

For the Ailsby kids, with love.—C.C.M.

AMICUS ILLUSTRATED and AMICUS INK
are published by Amicus
P.O. Box 1329, Mankato, MN 56002
www.amicuspublishing.us

Library of Congress Cataloging-in-Publication Data
Names: Miller, Connie Colwell, 1976- author. | Assanelli, Victoria, 1984- illustrator.
Title: You're in trouble : fib or truth? / by Connie Colwell Miller ;
  illustrated by Victoria Assanelli.
Description: Mankato, MN : Amicus. [2018] | Series: Amicus illustrated.
  Making good choices
Identifiers: LCCN 2016057208 (print) | LCCN 2017014637 (ebook) | ISBN
  9781681512532 (pdf) | ISBN 9781681511634 (library binding) | ISBN
  9781681522326 (pbk.)
Subjects: LCSH: Truthfulness and falsehood in children—Juvenile literature.
  | Decision making in children—Juvenile literature.
Classification: LCC BF723.T8 (ebook) | LCC BF723.T8 M55 2018 (print) | DDC
  177/.3—dc23
LC record available at https://lccn.loc.gov/2016057208

Editor: Rebecca Glaser
Designer: Kathleen Petelinsek

Printed in China
HC 10 9 8 7 6 5 4 3 2 1
PB 10 9 8 7 6 5 4 3 2 1

ABOUT THE AUTHOR

Connie Colwell Miller is a writer, editor, and instructor who lives in Mankato, Minnesota, with her four children. She has written over 80 books for young children. She likes to tell stories to her kids to teach them important life lessons.

ABOUT THE ILLUSTRATOR

Victoria Assanelli was born during the autumn of 1984 in Buenos Aires, Argentina. She spent most of her childhood playing with her grandparents, reading books, and drawing doodles. She began working as an illustrator in 2007, and has illustrated several textbooks and storybooks since.